THE CHAMELEON'S POISON

IURGI URRUTIA

Cover Photo by Iñaki Chico (Kontraluz Studio)

Print Edition Cover Design by Iurgi Urrutia, Iñaki Chico, Unai Arana

The Chameleon's Poison © Iurgi Urrutia. All Rights Reserved, except where otherwise noted.

To everyone and anyone who's ever lent me a book to read.

To libraries for giving me access to a diverse range of resources.

To librarians for wisely guiding me to new books, words and worlds.

To everyone who has ever shared their poetry, writings and scribbles with me.

To all my friends for putting up with me and always being there, rain, hail or shine.

To the Meadows family for always being supportive, generous and a positive force of nature.

To my brother and parents for instilling a deep love of books, theatre and art in me from a very young age.

To Anna and Beren for always weathering my storms with sunshine, supporting the madness with more madness of their own and always inspiring me to be better.

Through all the faces that we wear
Sometimes joy, sometimes despair
The mask has gone, no mystery
Replaced by fraud and trickery
Nathan's Phase (Mark's Songbook) – The Chameleons

How many years since you found yourself
Staring at an endless sky?
Unaware of yourself
Who you are and where you're going
Only living
Only breathing
Losing all sense of time
Endless Skies – VNV Nation

Among the countless writers and artists that have in some way or another influenced and inspired me for this book I want here to pay particular tribute to Blas de Otero, Mario Benedetti, Eliseo Subiela and his *The Dark Side of the Heart*, Franz Kafka, The Chameleons and VNV Nation.

Most importantly, this book would never be what it is now and it would never have been completed, without Dean Marando and Anna Meadows, to whom I'm highly indebted.

Prologue

He was feeling much better, his skin was regaining its rosy colour, and his eyes no longer looked empty and tired. He always seemed strong and in control, even the first day I arrived, before the operation. It was not pride, it was simply that he didn't want to worry anyone; he hated people fussing about him.

"I'll have to go down to the garage and see the car," I said.

If there was something in the world that he loved more than Mum, it was that car. It wasn't an antique, not in the sense of the 1935 three and half litre Bentley, but he owned an early Peugeot 404 model and despite being more than fifty years old, it still looked brand new.

Over the last few years the car had been sitting in the garage, unused, but he still went down to visit his old friend every single day to lovingly wipe away the dust of the last twenty four hours.

"I sold it," he said. There was no bitterness in his voice, just a simple fact stated plainly. But his eyes darkened for a second.

I didn't know how to respond, what to say, so I simply stared at him looking for answers.

"I could not take her out, and I could not ask more of Thomas, so I sold it."

The first thing I realised was that he referred to the car as *it* when speaking of the sale, but spoke of *her* when he referred to his time with the car.

Good old Thomas was our neighbour, he was only a kid when he moved into the neighbourhood and father bought the car. Now that the old man couldn't take care of *her* any more, Thomas took it upon himself to take the car out once a week to keep the engine alive.

"Did he buy it?"

"Who? Thomas?" He asked and I nodded. "No. I offered it to him, but he wouldn't take it. He said, that it wouldn't feel right for him to own her. And you live so far away, what was I…"

"So who did you sell it to?" I interjected.

"Thomas didn't want it, and no one in the family wanted it. They said it would feel wrong to be driving her. At the same time, I wanted her to be cared for."

"I'm glad you sold it, I told you long ago… that car and you are the same. I can have you without the car, but I could not have the car without you. I couldn't bear it."

He smiled.

I had travelled half way across the world thinking that I would not have time to say goodbye, thinking that, perhaps, I was travelling to attend a funeral. Instead, I saw the man that had always worked from sunrise to sunset without a complaint, with a smile.

The operation had agreed with him. He was back.

"I received better offers, but it wasn't about the money. I sold it to the man that I thought would take care of her best. And I made sure he lived far enough so no one in the family would ever see her again."

I could sense it in his voice, I could see it in his eyes, but the question came out unconsciously. "You miss her?"

He turned to me with that generous smile I had always loved. "Son, sometimes you have to let go of the people and things you love most. That was a hard lesson to learn, but I learned it with you. It was for the best."

We were no different to any other father and son. We had our ups and downs, everyone does. His words moved me beyond what I thought was possible. I stood up and embraced him.

I wrapped my arms and body around him. So many years living on the other side of the world had deprived me of his presence, he had almost become a memory, but at that moment, his warmth, his body, felt like a perfect fit.

"I'll come back tomorrow morning," I said as I unwrapped my arms and took a step back. "Do you want me to bring you anything?"

"Don't worry," he said. "You're doing enough."

3 The Chameleon's Poison

I never saw him again. He left the world quietly, without a fuss, making sure that he died the same way he had always lived.

I was sitting at the top of the hill on the outskirts of the city when they called me with the news. The sea breeze caressed my skin. I took a deep breath and felt the familiar smell of the oak trees and the salt of the ocean. This was where I grew up, this was the place that formed me, that held most of my memories, but somehow, I knew it wasn't home any more; not to me.

It was then that something caught my attention. Sitting on a little pile of dirt, the familiar green glass of an apple cider bottle glimmered in the sun and I was compelled to pick it up.

The warmth of the sun on the glass spread through my fingers and it struck me that this wasn't an ordinary bottle; there was something special about it.

I noticed that a lot of papers with very small, fine writing filled it. I couldn't understand and still don't understand how they filled the bottle with all those papers. It seemed impossible but somehow they stuffed them all inside with words that I sensed could be important.

I walked home filled with anticipation and a sense of fate. I couldn't shake off the feeling that those words, those scribbles, had been written for me.

Once home, I broke the glass in the sink, retrieved the papers and laid them out on the table.

Whoever had stuffed all the notes inside the bottle had done a methodical and judicious job. All the writings were numbered, making the job of sorting them out incredibly easy. With all the pages in order, one small piece of torn paper stood out. Unnumbered, untitled, torn. It didn't feel part of the whole, but it had also come from the bottle.

The note contained three single lines that had undoubtedly been written by the same author. The characteristic, fine and elaborate writing style was there, but the page was ripped, slightly stained, and it was obvious that the writing was rushed. The letters were not as neatly formed as in the rest of the pages.

Vagabonds of undying souls
We wander the streets
Like ships without a sail

The words were fitting, the events of the last few days had stirred emotions long buried deep inside. I felt homeless in my own hometown. It had grown so much so rapidly that outside of the old town, I roamed the streets not knowing where I was going. Like a ship without a sail.

The pages called me back from my thoughts. Curiosity demanded that I read it all but I hesitated. The turmoil in my mind, my grieving heart, would not be healed by mysterious poems.

The pages called me again. It wasn't just curiosity, I had to know what I'd found. What it all meant.

I put the small, loose note to the side and braced myself to read the first poem.

I

The serenity of surrendering to an unknown ocean
Rearranging our fears
Leaving behind all the tears
Of unwanted yesterdays
Of burnt out, yearned for hideaways
Staring at endless skies
That blind our souls and illuminate our hearts
What would we be without a sun to cover our tracks?
What if we didn't wear masks?
Would we die in the corner of the world
Or would we blossom in ways unknown?

II

I could give you a piece of me…
My mind, my thoughts, even my devotion
I could give you all I possess
If you only allowed me to reach you

It's such a quiet ocean now
No roaring waves, no wrecked ships…
And yet you continue to send machines
To drag the sand, to widen the distance
You betray your shores, you burn your mountains
To move further from me

I burn the diary pages that tell
Your darkest side, your violent self
To make smoke signals that fill the sky
Do you see them in your distant shore?

…and you still send the machines
I hear them in the wind

What else do you want from me?
When all I give… a greener grass
Clear blue skies, my whole heart
Is not enough

What am I to do?
Would my life fill yours?

III

We flew across the lake of tears
Beyond the iron gates of oblivion
Past the cold caves of denial

We flew with heart-broken wings
Below the dome of bruised hopes
Past the high cliffs of hatred

We flew over the shelter of the poor
Opening our nest to all who'd come
In a warm spirit of solidarity

We flew beyond the grey horizon
Past the sandy pillars of history
Into the ashes of emptiness

IV

I've heard we are beautiful when we come into the world
That in the eyes of the newborn, glistens the light of the unknown
In their lips blossoms the smile of one who fears but is joyful
In their bodies burns a new spark and fire
And their heart holds a fertile land of new seeds

But I see an ancient wisdom in their eyes
A fire that will be filtered and turn stale through the years
A seed that will die dry and cold, in solitude
A seed that together with others will turn the field into a cemetery

V

Where are you sister?
You disappear in your silences
You vanish and I can't find you
I seek words that will reach you
I seek feelings that may awaken you
I meditate and concentrate on your being
But Destiny keeps us apart

Where are you sister?
In the dark nights of winter
Do you cry for times long gone
Or do you seek the smiles we've lost?
Do you still write your dreams and nightmares
Your joys, worries and woes?
The bond between us is unbreakable, eternal
But Time keeps us in our throes

Where are you sister?
They tell me you'll never come back
That you went somewhere else
That you left the Earth behind
You raised the sails on your ship
And now yearn for new shores
Always exploring new ports
Forgetting our past lives

Where are you sister?
That my words don't reach you
And are lost in oblivion
In the senseless void of emptiness
You left me behind and I look for you
I ask rivers, valleys and trees
Oceans, high skies and seas
They know nothing and I weep

Where are you sister?
I miss your profound words
Your caress, your thoughts
Your verses that heal my fears
I hope that someday you'll be back
And you'll draw words in the wind
That will fly to find me
And fill the emptiness I feel

When I don't have your words

VI

When the night hits the ground and scatters yesterdays
I will find you under the street lamp where we never met
Bringing light to the shadows surrounding
Breaking away from the furtive burning

When the sun hits the ground and scatters tomorrows
You will find me inside the cave where we never met
Bringing darkness to the light surrounding
Breaking away from the passive burning

VII

Words are never enough when it comes to this
They cannot truly express the depth and emotion
They can only convey on the surface what is felt
Deep inside the mystery that makes us ourselves

But, somehow, though inadequate, I must share
The difference you've made to this poor soul

Love it is not, if you take the easy road
If you simply go along without honesty
Love it is not, if you falter facing the storm
If you simply walk away without a fight

Uttering the words that others dare not
Keeping in check, pushing to the limit
The one who would otherwise not be fulfilled

Mastering waves of rage from the shore
Taming the tempest with rightful might
Care and trust until it embraces and surrenders

A tower, a lighthouse, a star…
I dream and you're here
In the shadows of my cave
Whispering my name
By my side

Warm, calm
Like Winter's morning sun

VIII

I seek you
Ever moving
Formless
Always changing
Your anger never tamed
Roaring from eternity
Your calm never surpassed
Inspiring tranquillity
Your many faces
Always honest
Always beauty
You are the beginning and end
The essence of life
From you we came
And in you we must end

IX

Do you see me
Among the war and noise?
I'm by your side
At the darkest time
And here I'll stand
With you
Silent
Still

You enter the dark tunnel
And run away
I'm by your side
At the darkest time
And you never see me
With you
Walking
Weeping

We enter the frozen lake
I lead the way
I'm before you
At the darkest time
Opening the path
With you
Frightened
Willing

When the sands of time
Come to an end
When all we know
As it came to be
In one single moment
Vanishes without a trace

15 The Chameleon's Poison

Here I will be
At your side
Invisible
Until the last ray of light dies

X

I waited in solitude at the traffic lights
Away from the dustbowl we called home
The wind danced with the wheat fields
Flirting with the ancient oaks surrounding
But avoided me as if somehow it knew
The thunderstorm contained within me
Clouds aided the moon to travel in hiding
Invisible to the eyes of a world of silence
Darkness was palpable in the land of honey
Where cruelty, like bread, was always baked
In the furtive hours before the red dawn
I waited in solitude but the train never came
The path vanished, like dust in the storm

XI

Winter's bitter tears
Fall on your hands
As you fall asleep
Embracing your silence
As days draw to an end
And stars glimmer down low
On our horizon and our land
But never up in the sky
How many promises crashed
Blind in the night without stars?
How many friends abandoned us
Weary and lost since birth?
Never ceasing
Uncertainty in motion
Stumbling here and there
Kissing and caressing us
With open eyes
Inviting us to create anew
Calm oceans
Caressing the rocks
Shaping their life
Their character
Their history

XII

Will we remember the warmth of the sun?
How it caressed our skin as we walked by the canal
When we were free

Will we remember the bitter cold of winter?
How it wrapped itself around us as we laughed
When we were young

Will our silences grow more meaningful
As the years go by?

A break

The room felt cold, my skin slightly clammy. As the sun had set, the temperature had fallen dramatically outside and had filtered into the room. For a moment I wished I could be a reptile so I could change my temperature accordingly.

I stood up and turned the kettle on. Despite the sound of light traffic filtering in through the window, a solemn and heavy silence filled the air. It was the silence of people. There were no voices, no shouts, no signs of life apart from traffic. It struck me that it was dark, it was cold, but the street shouldn't be this quiet.

The soothing sound of the kettle starting to boil filled the room as I walked to the window and lowered my gaze to the street below. The hostel was next to the main square and the sight of a couple of hundred people holding candles explained it all. The silent vigil had muted everything. Only machines continued with their noise unaware of the solemn human emotions the vigil evoked.

The banner they had laid out on the ground piqued my interest. It read: *No more deaths. Asylum is a right. Refugees welcome.*

I smiled.

I'd been born in exile, unaware of the situation but away from the home of my ancestors. My father, a refugee had to leave it all behind, running for safety.

The smile widened as I realised that Maya would be down there. She had to be. Whenever there was a cause, whenever there was a chance of lending a hand or changing things for the better to those most in need, Maya was always first in line.

The water boiled, the kettle flicked itself off. Suddenly, the hot cup of tea that I so desperately needed two minutes ago felt irrelevant. A new warmth filled me inside as I picked up the phone and dialled with anticipation.

"Maya, it's me. I'm in town," I said, feeling a little awkward.

Maya and I had been inseparable all through childhood. Even when we attended different high schools and many of our friends left us along the way, we had always remained together. In a world of constant change, our relationship had been as strong and certain as the sun in the sky.

When I left the city, I didn't just leave the streets that had made me who I was. I didn't just leave my family behind. I left her. And that had been the hardest. Could a person survive without oxygen?

Somehow, I did. We did.

Adaptation. Who knows! We had learned to live without each other.

Maya continued building her social work, unabated by a world that seemed to be breaking at the seams. The degradation of the environment, wars for oil, waves of terrorism, a financial crisis, the betrayal of the European promise, the erosion of the social fabric, could not deter her will.

I travelled, roamed the earth and settled almost on the other side of the globe. Sometimes she joked if part of me needed to escape the life I had to build a new one as far away as possible. Had there been a plan or did it just happen by chance?

Whilst we communicated by text messages and emails regularly, we seldom talked on the phone. My voice must've seemed distant and unfamiliar. Furthermore, I hadn't told her I was coming.

"Sorry, to call out of the blue," I apologised.

"It's okay," she replied, slightly cold, a little awkward, still grappling to come to terms with the surprise. "I'm just in the middle of something but we must meet. Can I call you back?"

The warmth in her voice had returned.

"Are you at the vigil?" I asked.

Holding a candle, standing by her side, it seemed like nothing had changed. Two decades later and here we were, shoulder to shoulder, hoping for a better, kinder world. I'd only arrived for the last few minutes of the vigil but it felt good to be there.

21 The Chameleon's Poison

People withered away and we started walking. There was no need for words between us. We both knew where we were going.

The Old Station Pub was central to our lives. We had spent far too many hours discussing everything from the most vulgar to the most sacred inside its dark and musty walls as we watched trains arriving and leaving, families reuniting and saying goodbye.

"When's your next book coming out?" She asked as soon as we each had a pint in front of us. "I want more. The world needs to hear more from you."

I shook my head in response. "I wish…" I muttered under my teeth with sadness. "I haven't written anything for years Maya. Sorry to disappoint but there's no big opus on the horizon."

"I thought…" she began but I chuckled with bitterness and her words died in the air.

"Whenever I manage to put a few words together they end up in the bin. It seems I just don't have anything else to say."

Her eyes scrutinised me like a CT scan scouring for answers.

"How come you're back?" She asked changing the topic.

A shadow darkened my brow. This wasn't just the defeated resentment of a once prolific writer, it was something deeper and she sensed the depth and turmoil inside me as vividly as a needle piercing through the skin.

She always knew how to read me. Nothing could ever be secret between us.

Her hands took mine. Her eyes offered a light, a spark, like a lighthouse in the dark.

I felt safe.

"The old man passed away this afternoon."

There was no point in saying anything else. Maya turned and wrapped her arms around me for what felt like eternity.

She never let me go.

I needed her strength, her warmth, and she wanted me to know that she would always be there for me. She wouldn't let me go until I was ready to face the world again.

Lost in her embrace, wrapped in her cocoon, time, space, life and death all seemed inconsequential.

I turned the kettle on.

Her warmth still lingered in my heart but the bitter cold outside remained fixed on my skin. I leaned against the bench and thought about Maya's ability to always remain hopeful, to keep heading towards the horizon even if it never felt any closer, struggling against every obstacle but still marching on.

The world's problems had a way of becoming my own. They affected me so deeply that I grew bitter, angry, hateful. Years of action that had changed nothing had taken their toll on me. She never gave up.

The kettle flicked itself off bringing me back to the room. I had a way of getting lost in my thoughts.

My gaze returned to the papers lying on the table. I emptied the cold tea that had been waiting there for the last four hours and replaced it with a steamy one.

The hot tea soothed my throat, its steam gave me comfort and I readied myself to continue reading.

XIII

I want you to love
Without pretence
With brutal honesty

I want you to love
Without craving
With desire burning

I want you to love
Without gains
With trepidation and fear

I want you to love
Without limits
With unrestrained will

I want you to love
The way you hate

XIV

Cherish who you were
Before they burned
The core of your being
In order to control
The way you live
The way you walk
The way you talk

They take you by the hand
To their promised land
But look at the void you leave behind
Where your brothers lived and laughed
Where your sisters lived and cried
Silence and decay where there was joy

We bark at nights of oblivion
Smothered by vain hopes
We search for the horizon of our lives
With horses of steel that run
Under the shadow of heaven
Leading nowhere the mass of the forgotten

You see...

We've got history too
Maligned, never aligned with their version of the event
Bruised, ever abused within the confines of their rent
We've got history too
Rendered invisible by those who profess their love
By those who torture the dove from above

Once more, the night curtains torn
Blindness reigns the land of stars
Afraid of the future, denying the past
Dreams vanish before they're born

25 The Chameleon's Poison

Once more, the thin line is drawn
Iron shackles of hearts and minds
Chains of slavery lost in time
When hope is lost and gone

Once more, our voices are drowned
Power and dominion from above
Dictating what's hate and what's love
Fading into a cacophony of sound

Once more…

Faith overcomes the lost souls
In machines that feed off fear
With wretched minds that beggar belief
You, spiteful soul, feed off
The broken wings of angels

Fly beyond the towers of smoke
And tell me there's joy in the eyes of sorrow
Tell me there are bridges in the sand dunes
Tell me there's life at the tip of the arrow

Wake me up from this slumber
Whisper your worries at night
Cover my body with ashes
Bury our disagreements
We're the ocean
The spring and river
We're the mountain
The meadow, the sky

To live as if dying
To lie as if living
To smile as if lying
To stay as if leaving

XV

The sun filters in through the blinds
Will I ever find one
That prevents light from entering my room?
It's dawn on our side of the world
And trams have started their daily pilgrimage
How does one wake up from a night of sleepless insomnia?
I know, I had a book somewhere…

A million ideas cross my mind
While everybody else lies in their healing sleep
Could I leave all this behind?
Could I vanish never to return?
Could I just switch off my mind?
Goodbye…

Do you remember how it used to be?
Every little thing we enjoyed…
Giggles, tears, a smile
The rain, the snow, the sky

A little backyard would become
A kingly palace of days of old
With thousands of hectares of land
With jugglers, bards and miraculous wizards
In our gentle hands

But now you're kidnapped every morning
You disappear and I'm left wondering
Do you know where they take you?
Sometimes your eyes seem red, hollow
Bloodshot, swollen
Sometimes you look as weary, as frail
As a one hundred year old
Your lips cracked and dry, your hair
Sticky, your breath rotten

27 The Chameleon's Poison

Your body pale like the fresh snow
In the Arctic, your body cold

Every night they release you back
Thrown onto the front nature strip
Each purple bruise counting
One kidnap, one release

Where once there was joy
There is nothing but death
Silence and death
Where once stood
An oak and an elm
And a stream of fresh spring water
Now there's a wasteland

Once I cared, I empathised, I felt…
Now he is dead and I feel nothing
I see the corpses scattered in the streets
And I don't care, I feel nothing

I've become the monster I always feared
The monster that filled my dreams
That wove my nightmares
The one I never wanted to be

So I cleanse my empty nothingness
In boiling water
As my skin bubbles and burns

I distance myself…
I sit down to meditate
Leave my body behind
I need time to think
I need time to reach
The child
I need to hear the dispossessed cry
But when I'm back
I find my body battered, shattered
The skin peeled, muscles torn
Bones protruding in a thousand directions

Like the skeleton of a bombarded city
Surrounded by a sea of blood
Deep red blood, cabernet sauvignon
Aromatic and fruity, sweet and lazy
Yet, enduring and strong

I cleanse my empty nothingness again
In boiling water
And my skin bubbles and burns
Swells, breaks, bursts
A thousand burns
A thousand wounds…
And the pus washes off
But there is no blood
Not in my dry wasteland
In this dead body
This shadow

Another sleepless night of insomnia
Empty trams, fields of carcasses
Swollen eyes, hoarse throats
Bloodied hands, bruised, beaten wives
Tearful accountants and lustful priests

XVI

If open hearts are to be slaughtered
If Jesus is to be awakened
If stock values are the measure of humanity
If torture is to be the welcoming party
Let us migrate to another land

If innocence is the crime of our days
If history must be riddled with deceit
If honesty can be bought for a cent
Let us not pretend there's a place for us

XVII

If only we could undo all of the things we've done
Take back the sorrow and pain we've caused
And rebuild the paths and bridges that were lost

If only we could withdraw bulldozers and chainsaws
Heal the virus that sent you to the wilderness
And recreate the seeds of open tenderness

If only we could enjoy and keep the silence
Immutable in our defiance and mourning
And feel the anxiety and anger burning

If only we could read the book of the future
Unlearn wisdom and embrace the unknown
Shedding tears for those who are gone

You see….

It doesn't matter how many times you bring us down
Because we'll rise again to your dirty, old nest of vipers
Our curse is to love you despite the poison you spit
Unconditional love for all the hate you feed
Weaving life and death, sorrow and joy, anger and pain
We thought we were the only ones
And we'd sacrifice it all for them
But your spores grow and spread
And we can see you'll never repent

It doesn't matter how many times you say you've changed
Because we know you will kill again when the time comes
Your curse is to hate despite all the love you get
Unbound fear for all that surrounds your nest
Weaving nightmares and dreams, hopes and despair
You're the only one to see
And you'll sacrifice it all
Killing with poison all that remains
Dead hearts filling your hall

31 The Chameleon's Poison

And the bitter salt of tears has thickened our skin
The deep well of pain has sharpened our senses

We're crying
We're fearing
We're dying
We're fading
And it's all in your mind

XVIII

The city awakes asleep
It grows and sprawls
Another road, another highway
It lives in future pasts
In embers of burnt hope
We shatter our own dreams
Before we even have them
We create vain hopes
And strive to destroy them
So afraid of the possibilities
That we close the roads
Building barriers where there were none
So ashamed we are
Of our human nature
That we try to fit into unreality
Building books of lies
Attempting to justify
Our unnatural acts

XIX

Traces of cobblestones
Hide the path, hide the past
Names and streets that were
Filled with life and joy
Once they stood free from grief
Free from sorrow and misery

I look at you when I know
You're not looking
I peel your skin with my teeth
Undressing your body
Revealing your secret

You shaved your head
You cut your nails
You bruised your lips
And ate your own meat

How did it feel?
How did it feel to taste
The hatred you inflicted
On others since your birth
How did it feel to rape
Your own being, afflicted
By loathing and mirth

You built a statue of yourself
An unreal illusion for others
To adore and gloat over
You built a mirage of yourself
A caring and nurturing goddess
That never accepted the other
You filled the streets with pestilence
Smothered hopes and violence

Cobblestones of your mind
Cobblestones and pain
Cobblestones and rain
Cobblestones and pain

XX

Lift your eyes
Face the hovering drones
The insolence of war
Shrouded in clouds
The gathering storm
That tears your soul
The beacon of light
A tapestry of deceit
Blinded
With bleeding eyes
Wandering
Aimlessly
Use my eyes to gaze
At the unseen

Whisperer of snakes
You learn the past
Was a wondrous mistake
Winter came too early
Our desire waned
All traces erased
In dying embers
Of a fading sun

I hear you cry behind the bars
Tears of guarded hope
I hear you through the storm
A song for the future to come
Hold on
Hold on to your roots
Let them grow strong
Let the killers come
Striking with a silence
That breaks the night

I'll kiss them
Soothe their hate
When they harvest
What they've sown

XXI

I wander through the paths
That tread the emptiness of your legacy
I wander not knowing why
The shadows of injustice you sowed
In autumn storms
Your eyes bleeding
Your pale voice in the wind
Your hunger never satisfied

Inland lighthouse
Crucible of cultures and people
Of voices, poetry and minds
They say you gave yourself to their arms
That they never subjugated you by the sword
You rejected your liberty for servitude
Your vast plains for a maze inside a cage
But if you embraced them and surrendered
What did they fear?

Tell me
What did they fear?

They toppled your towers
Your defences, your forts
Stone by stone
Pebble by pebble
They trampled your freedoms
Prosecuted your will and strength
Beyond the two sisters
The mountains and the ocean

What did they fear
If you had embraced them?

And now, centuries later
They keep piercing your mind
Eroding your tongue
Strangling your pride
Distorting your truth
(Which fits not with their lie)

Less than a century ago
You still preserved your self
But what's left of you?
Tattered country
Stolen and conquered
Tortured and shattered
Your virtues and wisdom
Your history and words
Rest silent in the past

Of the kingdom
Only the word remains
Empty of content
Without meaning
Stone by stone
Pebble by pebble

XXII

How did we lose the dream
And let it slip away unnoticed?
How did we lose the hope
And let it grow strong with fear?

When did we become so cold, so numb
That we crawl through the days in chains of despair
With the broken apathy of a torn will?

When did we surrender to the depths
Of an emptiness that we cannot quite grasp
And to which we condemn our heart?

We walk through barren streets
With disposable hearts, souls and minds
We talk with unspoken words
That render us unable to ever read the signs

To ever stand up on our own and embrace
The earth, the wind

XXIII

I was waiting on the porch and you never came
We built our cabins together, shoulder to shoulder
I was waiting for you but you vanished in thin air

I sat in solitude and recalled the good old day
We built bridges and backdoors to link our cabins
I sat thinking of you and how you went astray

I was waiting on the porch and you never came
A loud rumble awakened me from a deep slumber
I was waiting and your cabin vanished in thin air

I sat in solitude and pondered if I should leave
Your cabin in ruins, mine, rotten and abandoned
I sat thinking of our loss and how to weave

A new destiny on my own
With all bonds now undone
Eyes far in the distance
Free from penance

XXIV

Reality is a mirage of our dreams
A constructed perception of our mind
Assumptions are all we ever have
As we build our lives night after night

And we murder the murdered
Rewriting and reinventing their legacy
Raping their lives and words without mercy
To keep marching ahead on our quest
To keep piling more bodies over theirs

We murder the murdered
And vanquished we roam the earth
Crawling through wastelands of death
Anguished we hide from the world
From the barren, the wild, the cold…
As we strip our hearts out
And feed them to the wolves
Until we find our peace

XXV

Give me the peace I yearn
Punch me in the face
So I know that I'm awake

Give me your warm embrace
Tighten your arms around my neck
So I know I'm not dead

Give me your sweet lips
Your poison in my veins
So I know who holds the reins

Give me your soft whispers
Speak the spell that smothers
So I know I'm still here

In this nightmare we share

XXVI

Identity, is the being of a self
The ever changing result of the traces
That the environment leaves on us since birth
The moving, living equation of the answers
To our sentiments, life, smiles, and memories
We don't choose ways of thinking
We absorb customs and voices
Assimilating them inside us, as we construct
New landscapes and forests

But careful
Not all mountains are the same
Not all changes are wrong
Movement is always constant
But the self can be shattered
And therein lies the risk
Because a torn identity
Makes for a lost being
One who instead of doing right
Will do wrongs of the rights

Where is the measure for normality?
How did the ill of hate come to be?

I would like the answers somewhere
The manual to the questions that pile up in my mind
The ability to understand the sense of senselessness

XXVII

It's always a masquerade in the heart of our land
And I always find myself without a costume
Apart from all the others and often on the run
While you dress up like a princess and wait
For the poisoned apple to come

But I
Today and always
Remember the acts of the past
How you were left in a dark street
By those who play the cruel game
Your dress in rags, fallen in your vomit
Trying to escape from yourself
Stirring your inside, bereft

Only my feelings for you can kill me
Their gentle words, state and cross
Fly over and vanish on the way to hell
You've broken me with your love
But tomorrow remember today
And escape from your torturing cell

Their silent words creep into my mind
And I start losing my identity
Love becomes a blur of the past
And I don't recognise the me in the mirror
The chameleon's poison runs through my veins
Awakening new feelings, changing my points of view

Suddenly I find myself in a strange land
With my being lost at their command

Never let nostalgia run the threads of your life
For that road is full of traps, death and lies

On my knees, shattered in the night
I feel a ray of light, the breath of your life

45   The Chameleon's Poison

And tonight, tonight I need you by my side
Your hatred, sorrow, and closeness
Your contradiction and sharpness

It seems strange to see the paleness
Of the moonflowers that blossom
In a free spirit like yours

Alone in a dark barren street
I listen for violent steps behind
Like titanic hammers at my feet
Only silence reaches my ears

Your voice comes then to my heart
Your eyes, green, cold, and dead
Your courteous and poisonous hand
When I get back home instead
Solitude and silence hit me in the face
Reminding me that I'm a prisoner of the sun

Drums again, far and distant
The call to war soars like a master
And children softly start to chant
Not knowing that someday they too
Will be like us

Over the drums, you and I
As usual, sing again the same song
Not daring to confront our being or addiction
Always hatred and discord, but together
Like those lustful lovers of ancient days
Making our living out of sin, somehow

You and I are the biggest traitors
Still pretending to be lovers
Wearing masks and holding hands
Confusion, the cry of our minds
While frustration boils over

But how to escape from here
When the neighbour is always staring at you?

How to scream? How to cry? How to try?
Imprisoned, in silence, in shadows

Not even knowing how we lost what we had
Afraid of all the others, always wearing masks
It's them who control our thoughts, feelings, and beings
Entering our flesh until they're one
Until we lose our identity and past
Until we are what they want

He wasn't the only one to die on that cross
But thousands of men and women
And many, perhaps, wiser than the one
They love, glorify and adore

And while we keep probing for answers
We take care of the walls that protect us
Never letting anything in and never going out
So we never know what's outside
Building hollow hypothesises
Always changing and twisting everything
Placing ourselves above them
And caressing our four little walls

I place the cross on my shoulder
I see them, but they never see me
I fall to the ground
And they're always blind or look to the other side
I fall again
And they laugh or ran away, far

Their poisonous tongues feed my veins
Filling my need, creating the sense of truth
Making me love their written and invisible laws

I fall to the ground again
And this time I win
For their sins my penitence

47 The Chameleon's Poison

The masks they wear…
Sometimes hate, others hope
Sometimes murder, others love

A thousand shots on the streets,
The smell of blood in the heart…
And as the masks get worn down
I see clearer and sharper
Behind their silent eyes

Rivers of blood flow down the street
With the scum and filth of our sins
Reaching the cold and cruel ocean
Like many treasures of ancient days
Fallen in hatred, drowned in confusion

Don't tell me again "this is just a phase
And after the war the sun will be back
To caress and give warmth to our land"

At last their crimes fill the air
Today, I'll leave behind the cross
And I'll take my mask off
Revealing a pale head with no flesh
Showing the world the face
Of the brother they've murdered and raped

XXVIII

Kill me without mercy
Professing love to the four winds
Silence my voice
Talking of democracy and tolerance

Tear my being
Absorb me in your arid wasteland
Lie to me in wrath
Promising respect and liberty

Don't ever change
It's your poison which keeps me alive

XXIX

It was your love
Professed to the four winds
Which withered the clouds
Erased the road and the horizon
And silenced the voices of the future

It was your love
Professed to the four winds
Which buried the trees
Darkened the sun and the moon
And shed tears of salted honey

It was your love
Professed to the four winds
Which imprisoned thought
Chained the ice sheets
And elevated death to the heavens

It was your love
Professed to the four winds
Which forced stars to slumber
Harvested lies and bitterness
And dried the spring and the river

It was your love
Professed to the four winds
Which bled the oceans dry
Collapsed the sands of time
And toppled the gates of fate

It was your love
Professed to the four winds
Which taught me the value of silence
Reawakened in me a new conscience
And gave me hope for a new world

It was your love
Professed to the four winds
Which cut loose moorings with the past
Revived the deserts and wastelands
And brought new life to this dead heart

A pause

A sharp pain concentrating on my feet and numbing my legs pulled me out of the reading. I stretched them and walked up and down the room for a couple of minutes.

The poems felt like echoes of my own thoughts, my own struggles and turmoil; a mirage of my own self. But there was something else there; a lingering hope hiding just beneath the surface.

I took a final sip, washed the mug and left it on the rack to dry. It was late at night and the traffic had died down giving way to a peaceful, comforting silence that only the night could offer in the city.

The final set of poems waited for me and I was eager to keep going, to see what they had to say.

XXX

I don't hold any truths in my life
I build theories and hypothesises
Always searching, tirelessly
For the answers that will enrich them

How long will you continue
To insult and slander those who don't agree with you
Those who don't share your views
Denying and vanishing them from your world

It's easier to somehow hold on
To one simple truth
To protect a strongly built ship
In a familiar and calm sea

But I prefer to sail
An unknown twisted ocean
And reach new shores
In an enquiring fragile boat

XXXI

Time and space
An infinite universe
Separate us
But our memories will endure
As stars glimmer in the night

Paradise and heaven
A thousand silences
Separate us
But our words will endure
Latent in the caves of winter

Longing, desires and love
Days, nights and years
Separate us
But our dreams will endure
While we aim for new utopias

XXXII

They wanted us to give up on our future
To shed all we had achieved through the years
To reject all that we had gained through blood and tears

They wanted us to vanish into oblivion
To willingly erase our own history and existence
To surrender to their deadly will without any resistance

We roamed the earth as if there was no tomorrow
They said we'd die through misery and sorrow
Treading lost paths until we formed our burrow

And in our shelter
Away from all danger
Distant from the world
Marooned from fate
Stranded from space and time
Scrapped from history
Erased from memories and timelines
We surrendered the fight
We embraced the light

The ever changing uncertainty of life

XXXIII

Letting go of anger and pain
The hatred deep inside
That corrodes our mind
Raising the anchor
Floating on the surface
Dancing with the currents
Without desire, without pride

We still remember how you stopped the bleeding
Turned away despair and brought back the sun
Yours were our lives, ours souls, our hearts

We still remember how you offered a new path
Proclaiming the right to dream a new horizon
Ours were your eyes, your words, your smiles

We'll build a humble new home on your return
The wasteland is no place for a giving heart like yours

XXXIV

I can see deep behind your eyes
Hidden and silent in your mind
The faint mirage of our youth
The shining, rusty burden of our past
Do you believe now, as I stand before you
As our hearts resume our old conversation
That back then, we had freedom within our reach?
That what we did was nothing but treason?
And we both know love was driving us
But how did we rip apart what was so important
So essential in our own lives?

Why did we part ways
You taking one path and I the other?
As if there were only two paths to tread
Do you think that we lost our hearts then?
Do you think that our hearts were sick
Dirty, vanquished, bruised, boiled over?

You took the path of poison wholeheartedly
Until the sun's rays burnt your skin
I took the path of silence and solitude
The rotten streets of the city footpaths
Making solitude law
Solidarity
Amity
Tears
Life…

XXXV

Your golden locks have lost their splendour
Falling black onto your white shoulders
Your eyes glimmer with the same light of youth
Like the lighthouse of calm I always perceived
The breeze of hope I always loved

They say that you're mortal
You abandoned the path of the gods
Took fate in your hands
And focused on the creation of life
That you drank from the well of tears
And created a new ocean in your likeness
Serene and deep, crucible of a thousand joys

Your golden locks have lost their splendour
Falling black onto your white shoulders
Shadows cover the earth and the sky
But in you survive: faith, love and hope

XXXVI

Undress my frailty under the moon
Caress me again like you used to do
Long ago, in the safety of our cocoon
Whisper the words that soothed me
Digging our sorrows with a silver spoon

How can I ask you
All the things I never thought of asking?
How can I ask you
All the things that need remembering?

I want to rediscover
Your gentle caress
Your strong embrace

I want to feel again

XXXVII

How to explain what we don't understand?
How to explain the turmoil in our minds?
We wear masks of joy not to upset the other
We are chameleons of many innocent faces
Just to see their smile, to enjoy a momentary glimmer

Why do we not like ourselves?
Why do we sabotage our lives?
Yearning always for what's out of reach; a dream, a lie
A lie, I say, because the dream is a mirage
A mirage that keeps us moving forward, struggling
Through the dunes, the treacherous sand, the desolate path
The wasteland that surrounds us and we carry in our hearts

It's not fair for you to bear the burden, the cross
Every eight years the same sorrow, the same loss
It's not fair I say, and still you shimmer
To this wasteland, this confused swimmer
Who never reaches a shore

I want to make you proud, I want to be strong
After all there would be no sun in the sky
If a shadow came between us
But fear consumes me from within
Fear of my own hopelessness
Fear that the wasteland is too big
Too dry, too dead, too gone
Fear of what I already am
And what I may become
Fear of my weaknesses
Fear that we will mourn
The past we had, the days of yore
That only our memories will endure

And still, I see your sun and my doubts vanish, dissipate
Like dew, like morning fog on a sunny, Autumn day

XXXVIII

Belonging
Being part of
A shared purpose
A voice
An understanding

Growing roots
Within the forest
Stretching arms
Both to earth and sky
Expanding branches
Following the way
That opens all paths

Questioning
Finding light
Where shadows hide
Where fears and hopes lie

Fighting
To right the wrongs
Healing
The injustices
That never end
Loving and caring
The freedom they murdered

Breaking
Temples and templates
Walking away from being numbered
Claiming the past
Clawing the lust
Breaking
From the flock that drowns

XXXIX

What would night be without day?
A river without water
A heart without blood
A smile without joy
A theatre without an audience
A child without innocence
A tree without roots
A forest without life

What would a beach be without a sea?
A dance without feelings
A guitar without strings
A singer without a heart
A sky without stars
A poet without love
A glacier without ice
An ocean without a shore

What would I be without your presence?
Your breath and caress
Your joy and essence
Your will and warmth
Your gaze and longing

A hurricane without wind
A tower without foundations
A sinner without sin

XL

The Summer breeze caressed our skin
As we danced, surrendered, carefree
In the daze of early hours
Long before the first rays of the sun
And we built our home in the woods
Away from their prying eyes
Tending to our wounds
Embracing our hearts
Life was simple then
Before the storm

Ours were the dreams
The boundless possibilities
Free from the shackles
Of space and time
We shivered under the moonless night
Whispering words we never uttered before
And as the sun rose our voices soared
Singing melodies of old
Awakening the forest's soul

XLI

Despite the fears we held inside
We knew there was hope on the horizon
The salty breeze of the sea
Dancing in the waves carelessly
In the ocean we were born
On the plains we grew strong
Climbing mountains we greeted the sun
When we were young…

Despite the tears we held inside
We knew there was joy on the horizon
The high plains and snow peaks
Every stride a step with boldness and will
On the road we kicked the sand
On the mountain we did stand
As we roamed we learned to belong
When we were one…

Despite the hate we held inside
We knew there was love on the horizon
The treacherous valleys and cliffs
That we embraced with generosity
Giving shelter to those in the cold
Giving hope to those who were sold
Sharing our hope of a future to come
When we were old…

Despite the sorrow I held inside
When you passed away beyond the horizon
The desert of silence and grief
An oasis for all the future seeds
Creating anew from what was destroyed
Forging new suns where there was a void
Fostering new dreams to be enjoyed
When you were gone

XLII

We walked the forest
Unaware of the future
Holding hands
Singing to each other

We walked the forest
Building hypothetical futures
That stood proud and tall
On moving sands

Sharing our shadows
We unearthed our humanity
The imperfection of our pasts
As we embraced eternity

XLIII

Shattering our shackles we reached the sky
Dreaming of stars in the night
You came to me and I was free

We created our sun, we embraced the night
Our whispers slipped and faded
Our sorrows stale and jaded

I tried to reconcile our immortality
Every waking moment of tranquillity
Always entangled… unafraid, unashamed

The echo of our heartbeat vanished
The warmth of our caresses perished
And we're still here… awakened, aware

Within us joy and tears
Dreams, hopes, and fears
A boundless future
A utopia

XLIV

I offer you paths of ashes
For your steps to get lost
Like night when day comes

I offer you parchments of lies
For your eyes to get lost
Like waves in the sand

I offer you seeds of smiles
For your existence to shine
Like clouds at the summit

I offer you all, nothing, my life
For your heart to shine
Like the sun when day comes

XLV

Immerse your joys in my wounds
Drown your eyes in tears of salted honey
Look at me when my eyes are lost in the distance
Talk to me when, exhausted, I lie in deep slumber
Your smile my shadow, your spring my sorrow

Our silences fill spaces
Distance pushes us close to the abyss
And time drives us to oblivion
Mortals at destiny's mercy
Shipwrecked of senseless oceans
Storms come
We are lost in the fog
And still, here we are

XLVI

Echoes of our presence will remain
Afterthoughts of our speech and song
Defying the shades of space and time
That we have surrendered to for so long

In the embers of a winter long solitude
We will recall a glimpse of our past
The remaining traces of a warm embrace
Doomed from the start to never last

The mist will guide the ship that was lost
Fading into view, bringing back dreams
And we're still, ever hopeful, on the pier
As the world slowly breaks at the seams

They never wanted us to be ourselves
Forcing us to surrender to their iron chain
Betraying our identity for their masquerade
But here we stand free from regret and pain

Still young
Still reckless
Still ourselves
Still humbly holding on to our being

XLVII

Truths vanish with age
Uncertainties grow
But still…
We row and row
Through storms
Calm oceans and
Mountains of waves
Unable to find a port
Until we reach
The final unknown shore
As we learn of our ignorance
We let the ship take its course
Commanding less
And finding peace
Assured that whatever is faced
Will be overcome

XLVIII

The ocean lay me on the sand
As the sun set on the horizon
Alone, shivering, I sought a light
Leaving behind the shoreline
I grew under the comforting shade
Of the forests and mountains
Never afraid of the beasts surrounding
Never afraid of the winds roaring
Never afraid of the dark shadows haunting
But always, always yearning
For the wild waves crashing
By the sand
By the shore
By the ocean
Where I was born
And come the end
Where I will go

XLIX

We conquered the mountain they said didn't exist
We ascended holding hands through barren paths
We climbed with undying smiles as the sun burned our skin
Leaving behind the rubble of hardened, humble, gentle people
Abandoning our ancestors' foundations

Constructing a new future
Embracing uncertainty
Conquering unreachable horizons
Creating from the void with sparks
Dreams they said were impossible

We had the answers
Clear, sharp, attractive
We conquered horizons
Without sweat, with confidence

We lost the answers
Only questions remained
Deep in the valley, deep in slumber
Under the shadow of ignorance

And back at the harbour
We weighed anchors
Naked before the tides
We freed ourselves
Surrendered to the swaying
We danced mind to mind
Under the dark clouds
Among fortune and misfortune
Until our feet reached a new shore

We elevated our voices
Throughout valleys, mountains and cities
Breaking millenary silences
Creating sparkles from sand

73 The Chameleon's Poison

Proud towers from stone
Giving ourselves to the earth
Submerging ourselves
In the ocean of bliss
Free of misgivings

Without surrender, never forgetting
Waiting for what the future may bring

L

We open our wings even though we can't fly
We open our eyes even though light blinds us
We caress the future taunting the past
We exhaust our time until death comes

From the woods to the desert
From the clouds to the ground
From the mountains to the ocean
From nothingness to the void

LI

Sit down and observe the hustle and bustle
Let the sands of time go like a waterfall
Let the sun warm and caress your whole
Let the noise fill the echoes of your soul

Sit down on the side of the celebrations
Uninvited but more than a guest of the moment
Unreadable but always open to the present
Unheard but a voice that breaks the silence

Sit down and give yourself the chance
To make it through days, weeks, months and years
To grow through anger, joy, grief, love and tears
To build a world that mirrors you without fears

Sit down and reach out above the clouds
Crossing the gates of darkness into the light
Breaking the chains of power without a fight
Claiming as yours the blue sky and the night

Sit down aware of yourself and others
Unafraid of the shifting sand dunes of change
Unmoved by empty promises lost in the haze
Unfazed by the immutable dictates of fate

And when despair comes around the bend
When anxiety pummels your head
When uncertainty feeds off your will
Like an army of termites devouring a tree

Sit down and remember your dreams
Sit down and forge a bright new sun
Burst into a song
Build new paths

LII

It was the darkest of nights
We cuddled together like ancient cobblestones
Sharing, giving each other whatever warmth we had

It was a moonless night
No stars, no light, nothing but the bleakest shadow
The flicker in our eyes a lighthouse for the wasteland

It was the coldest of nights
Wind and fire froze like icebergs of olden times
Our hope in flames, the undying lands withstood

We remained
We survived
Our warmth
Our light
Our will

A new day
A new life
A new land

Epilogue

As I finished reading the last words, I became aware of the silence and stillness around me. I didn't know what to do, what to think. The poems had stirred something deep in my heart and mind.

I felt pain, but not in a bad sense. More like a gentle soothing pain that increased my awareness of myself.

My surroundings disappeared then and I stared at emptiness. A void opened before me and I sought to find an answer to the questions swirling in my mind.

I wanted clear, straight answers. Who wrote those poems? Why? Who was The Chameleon? Did the writer die poisoned? What did he, or maybe she, go through to write such bitter and sorrowful words? And yet, a longing for a new horizon filled the writing; beauty and hope were there.

Suddenly, the void disappeared and I returned to my cold, musty room. A pang of sharp pain had brought me back.

Pins and needles. Cold feet.

Who knows how long I'd been lost in my thoughts. The poetry-filled papers were still in my hands.

The sun had long disappeared in the far west and night asserted itself past midnight, conquering the city streets, while the house turned colder still.

Standing up from the chair, cautiously, I attempted to resurrect my feet and entered the kitchen to prepare another hot cup of tea.

Those raw poems had awoken feelings and emotions long buried.

The kettle boiled and I filled the mug to the top enjoying the scent of peach, orange and cinnamon. With the hot cup in my hands I felt the warmth instantly spreading from my hands and across my body. I gripped the mug stronger still, wrapping my hands around it until they almost burned.

The first sip felt like a nectar my body had been longing for since ageless times. Warm and content, I approached the window.

Epilogue

The streets were dark and empty. No one walked the footpaths and no cars rolled down the humid road. It was the wind, the rain, the cold, that filled the city with a tangible presence.

I had seen that street a million times before but it looked and felt different then as the chameleon's poison ran through my veins.

The telephone's ring awoke me.

"Hello," I managed to utter.

"Chameleon's have no poison," a strange and alien voice said.

"What...?" I responded and paused. "Who are you?"

"Don't forget," he said. "The poison's in your mind. The chameleons' strength is in the masks they wear."

"Who are you?" I asked confused. "Did you write those poems? Did you leave them there for me?"

A long silence stretched to what seemed an eternity but I could still hear him breathing. I could almost feel it through the telephone line.

"You're fire, life and fate. That is all," he said as the line died.

I dropped the phone on the table with my mind racing. Too many questions were left unanswered but a new determination, a new light filled me. I could sense a familiar old energy flowing through my veins.

"I've missed you," I thought to myself as I took a seat, pulled out a blank piece of paper and grabbed a pen.

What had once been as natural as breathing, had been as scarce as water in the desert for the last few years.

With the moon as my witness, silence as companion, my mind empty... my hand started to write.

The spring was flowing again.

Because...

Because there are no nights without moon and stars, even when they're obscured by clouds

Because the sun always rises driving darkness away, even after the darkest nights

Because rain will pour down to bring back to life the arid wasteland that surrounds us

Because life and death are bound together like sun and moon, day and night, you and I

Because time marches on unstoppable and relentless, always at its own pace unaware of us

Because our choices pave the path, shape our fate; formless and ever changing

Because we learn from mistakes, grow through failure, rise after every fall as we carry on

Because we're free from shackles, rules and authority, like a playful summer breeze roaming wherever it desires

Because we are ourselves, who we were born to be, not who or what they want us to be

Because the wasteland will recover and turn green, bringing back to life everything that was destroyed, soiled, spoiled

Because dreams, utopia and fantasy will always bring better fruits than grounded rational reality

Because we drink the poison and turn it into water, washing away their stain, disarming their will

Because we throw away our masks, leave behind the chameleon's skin and embrace a new conscience, a new life

Because our creative minds will always overcome every obstacle as long as there's a dream, a will

Because we will always tear the chains of misery and cast away the dark clouds they bring

Because…

Iurgi Urrutia was born in Bayonne (France), speaks and writes in three languages (Basque, Spanish and English – this being his third), but not a word of French.

During his teenage years he wrote compulsively. Thankfully that material is either lost or buried six feet underground somewhere safe, where it will never be found.

Iurgi studied Media Arts, had a little stint at the BBC in London and even wrote and directed some short films. He worked as a teacher for a number of years that he describes as exhausting but unbelievably rewarding.

Currently residing in Mordialloc (Victoria), Iurgi works at a public library surrounded by and sharing his love of books. He spends his days reading and writing when he's not procrastinating binge watching TV series and movies.

The Chameleon's Poison is his first collection of poems in English.

Web: http://iurgi.com

Twitter: @iurgiurrutia

www.ingramcontent.com/pod-product-compliance
Lightning Source LLC
Chambersburg PA
CBHW020622300426
44113CB00007B/746